The
Ordinary
Woman

The Ordinary Woman

and Other Poems I Love

Compiled by

Kathleen Watkins

Gill Books

Gill Books
Hume Avenue
Park West
Dublin 12
www.gillbooks.ie

Gill Books is an imprint of M.H. Gill & Co.

978 0 7171 8642 6

Printed by ScandBook AB, Sweden

This book is typeset in Dolly Pro.
The paper used in this book comes from the wood pulp
of managed forests. For every tree felled, at least one
tree is planted, thereby renewing natural resources.

A CIP catalogue record for this book is available from
the British Library.

5 4 3 2

To our wonderful daughters, Crona and Suzy.
To my parents, Tom and Dinah, the best in the world.
To my educators, Mr and Mrs Monks, and the nuns at
my Dominican convent boarding school. They gave me
the interests and hobbies of music, art and literature
that I have had all my life. How can I ever thank them?

CONTENTS

INTRODUCTION

I COULDN'T IMAGINE my life without poetry. It has been a huge part of my life for so many years.

I love the way poetry can be about ordinary things – the everyday – so beautifully constructed and put together. I envy and admire the genius of people who can put life into a nutshell, who have the gift to capture it all in a few short lines.

My love of poetry, I suppose, began when I was in school. In those days we would have to learn off poems line by line. There was for me such beauty in the written word, something which is still true for me to this day.

Writer Alan Bennett talks about poems as being 'accessible' or 'popular'. I like to think of the twenty-two poems I have selected for this anthology as 'performable'. I have performed many of these poems at various occasions throughout my life.

They have travelled with me. They have been part of our holidays in Donegal over the last twenty-six years, where we've enjoyed walking with family and friends. These walks – long or short, often depending on the weather – would always lead to someone's home for an evening of singing, dancing, storytelling and poetry reading. We've had some wonderful times there – never a dull night! The poems you find here are those most requested and enjoyed at these evenings, and indeed at the many gatherings at our home in Dublin. Some of these poems I've read in forty-six venues around the country, to give my husband, Gay, a break in the second-half of his one-man stage show.

Within our own family, some of these poems have become so familiar to us that we've given them their own names. We call Rita Ann Higgins's 'The Deserter', for instance, 'The Shirts', and 'When You're Asleep' by Mary Dorcey has become known as the 'Mother/Daughter piece'.

Poets, in my opinion, have a special ear for language. They display such familiarity with rhythm and pace, flow and rhyme. There's a trick to what to put in and what to leave out. Poets have to work hard to find the right word: to know when to cut and move lines, perhaps keeping them to use again later. It's like having a painting and putting a frame around it.

Indeed, poetry must paint a picture for me to really enjoy it. Like in Seamus Heaney's 'When all the others were away at Mass'; in my mind I can see the kitchen, the boy and his mother, and I can hear the splash of the potatoes as they're peeled. I especially enjoy when poets write about the family. It's not just something they've made up, like a work of fiction. It feels so real. It comes alive. I'm so happy to include some of Heaney's work in this book. I once recited 'Mid-term Break' on *The Late Late Show*. Seamus was there that night. He thanked me for the performance and signed my copy of his book. He did a personal dedication. It was a very special moment.

Despite my connection to many of these poems, I believe there is a plane that poets go to that I honestly can't reach. I think most other people are the same. Poets, in my opinion, work on another level. Their understanding and passion for language goes far beyond our own – how they can manipulate words to make a stunning sentence, and convey so much in a simple line that it's a knockout. Sometimes I wish the poet were beside me so they could explain something. I'd like to say to them, 'Open the door for me, would you?'

But you don't need to understand it all. As I said, the best poetry paints a picture. They create images of very real things that we know and recognise – quiet moments with our families and loved ones, and celebrations of the extraordinary instances of the everyday. We may never fully understand what a poem means but, similarly, poets may never understand just how much pleasure their work gives us. I hope you find some pleasure in these poems, too.

Kathleen Watkins

July 2019

'

BRENDAN
KENNELLY

I ONCE MET Brendan Kennelly coming out the front gates of Trinity College, Dublin. I told him that I had taken his book, *Cromwell*, on holiday with me and that, while I had read it cover to cover, I had not understood a word of it! He replied, 'Sure I didn't understand it myself!'

As we spoke, he started to tell me about when he came to Dublin from Ballylongford, County Kerry, for the first time in the 1950s. Before he left, his father told him, 'You're going up there now to Dublin. Take it aisy,' before continuing, 'and if you can't, sure take it as aisy as you can!'

I once had the privilege and honour of sharing a reading with Brendan at Trinity College. I couldn't believe it when he called me on the phone and asked to share a reading, so as to give him a little break. Brendan had such mastery over his audience that day. He was so relaxed, so happy, asking the audience if they had written their own few lines of poetry. He invited people to come up on stage and read their work. He had such joy in people putting words on paper – it was wonderful to him.

I SEE YOU DANCING, FATHER

No sooner downstairs after the night's rest
And in the door
Than you started to dance a step
In the middle of the kitchen floor.

And as you danced
You whistled.
You made your own music
Always in tune with yourself.

Well, nearly always, anyway.
You're buried now
In Lislaughtin Abbey
And whenever I think of you

I go back beyond the old man
Mind and body broken
To find the unbroken man.
It is the moment before the dance begins,

Your lips are enjoying themselves

Whistling an air.

Whatever happens or cannot happen

In the time I have to spare

I see you dancing, father.

THE STONES

Worried mothers bawled her name
To call wild children from their games.

'Nellie Mulcahy! Nellie Mulcahy!
If ye don't come home,
She'll carry ye off in her big black bag.'

Her name was fear and fear begat obedience,
But one day she made a real appearance –
A harmless hag with a bag on her back.
When the children heard, they gathered together
And in trice were
stalking the little weary traveller –
Ten, twenty, thirty, forty.
Numbers gave them courage
Though, had they known it,
Nellie was more timid by far
Than the timidest there.
Once or twice, she turned to look

At the bravado-swollen pack.
Slowly the chant began –

'Nellie Mulcahy! Nellie Mulcahy!
Wicked old woman! Wicked old woman!'

One child threw a stone.
Another did likewise.
Soon the little monsters
Were furiously stoning her
Whose name was fear.
When she fell bleeding to the ground
Whimpering like a beaten pup,
Even then they didn't give up
But pelted her like mad.

Suddenly they stopped, looked at
Each other, then at Nellie, lying
On the ground, shivering.

Slowly they withdrew
One by one.

Silence. Silence.
All the stones were thrown.

Between the hedges of their guilt
Cain-children shambled home.

Alone,
She dragged herself up,
Crying in small half-uttered moans,
Limped away across the land,
Black bag on her back,
Agony racking her bones.

Between her and the children,
Like hideous forms of fear –

The stones.

Brendan Kennelly (1936) is an Irish poet and novelist. Born in County Kerry, he studied at Trinity College, Dublin, where he wrote his PhD thesis, and at Leeds University. Kennelly's work is grounded in the Irish-language poetic tradition, making particular use of the vernacular of the local communities in which he grew up. He has over fifty books of poetry to his name and has also published novels and plays. Now retired, he was Professor of Modern Literature at Trinity College. In 1996, he won the International Dublin Literary Award and, in 2010, received an Irish PEN Award.

RITA ANN
HIGGINS

RITA ANN HIGGINS is one of my favourite people. She is a no-nonsense type of person, with her feet planted firmly on the ground. When my husband, Gay, did his one-man stage show touring forty-six venues around the country, I read 'The Deserter' and it was always a firm favourite with audiences.

Rita Ann is a very real person. She's like your friend next door, or a loving daughter, and indeed like my own mother. She's also a great observer of people, and always notices the small details. She's also very funny and tells it like it is. She has the mind of a writer and a wonderful way of speaking.

THE DESERTER

He couldn't wait
just up and died
on me.

Two hours,
two hours
I spent ironing
them shirts
and he didn't even
give me the pleasure
of dirtying them,

that's the type
of person he was,
would rather die
than please you.

But in his favour
I will say this for him,

he made a lovely corpse.
Looked better dead
than he did in our front room
before the telly,

right cock-of-the-walk
in that coffin,
head slightly tilted back
like he was going to say
'My dead people.'

He couldn't wait,
never,
like the time
before the All-Ireland
we were going to Mass,

he had to have a pint
or he'd have the gawks, he said.
That's the type he was,
talk dirty in front of any woman.

No stopping him
when he got that ulcer out,
but where did it get him?
... wax-faced above
in the morgue
that's where.

He's not giving
out to me now
for using Jeyes Fluid
on the kitchen floor,

or stuffing the cushions
with jaded socks ...
and what jaded them?
Pub crawling jaded them,
that's what.

He's tight-lipped now
about my toe separators,
before this

he would threaten them
on the hot ash.

The next time
I spend two hours
ironing shirts for him
he'll wear them.

THE POWER OF PRAYER

I liked the way

my mother

got off her bike

to the side

while the bike

was still moving,

graceful as a bird.

We watched out for her

after Benediction.

It was a game –

who saw her head-scarf first,

I nearly always won.

The day the youngest

drank paraffin oil

we didn't know what to do.

All goofed round the gable end,

we watched, we waited,

head-scarf over the hill.

Knowing there was something wrong

she threw the bike down

and ran.

She cleared fences

with the ailing child,

Mrs Burke gave a spoon of jam,

the child was saved.

Marched indoors

we feared the worst,

our mother knew

what the problem was.

'Not enough prayers

are being said in this house.'

While the paraffin child

bounced in her cot

we prayed and prayed.

We did the Creed,

a blast of the Beatitudes

the black fast was mentioned,

the Confiteor was said

like it was never said before,

Marie Goretti was called

so was Martha,

we climaxed on the Magnificat.

After that it was all personal stuff.

I liked the way

my mother

got off her bike

to the side

while the bike

was still moving,

graceful as a bird.

For good neighbours with jam

for pope's intentions

for God's holy will

for the something of saints

the forgiveness of sins

for the conversion of Russia

for Doctor Noel Browne

for the lads in the Congo

for everyone in Biafra

for Uncle Andy's crazy bowel

for ingrown toenails

and above all

for the grace of a happy death.

Rita Ann Higgins (1955) is a poet and playwright from Galway, where she still lives today. She has published prolifically, including poetry collections and plays for the stage, radio and screen. Poetry collections include *Witch in the Bushes* (1988), *Throw in the Vowels* (2005) and *Ireland is Changing Mother* (2011), while her plays include *Face Licker Come Home* (1991) and *Down All the Roundabouts* (1999). She won the Peader O'Donnell Award in 1989 and has received several Arts Council of Ireland bursaries. She has held numerous writer-in-residence positions and is a member of Aosdána.

W.B. YEATS

I LIVE JUST a few doors down from where W.B. Yeats was born, and a ten-minute walk from the home of the late Seamus Heaney. Bronze busts of both these poets can now be found in Sandymount Green, one at either side of the park. What a wonderful legacy these two Nobel prize winners have left us.

Lady Gregory is renowned for recognising Yeats's latent talent, and for creating the space for him to work at Coole Park. She encouraged and challenged his work, so much so that he would later write of her: 'She so changed me that I live labouring in ecstasy'.

Yeats was endlessly mixing with artists, writers and other interesting people. He was very interested in the Japanese art of Noh, in masks and the occult. His brother Jack, the painter, was also a writer and wrote for the *Manchester Guardian*. He once wrote a piece about racing tin cans on a beach, which included the wonderful line: 'Isn't it a marvellous thing the way we do utilise the airs of heaven for the purpose of making tin cans gallop like greyhounds?'

Some of my favourite poetry by W.B. Yeats includes his love poems for Maud Gonne MacBride. It is a stirring, romantic body of work. The two poems I've chosen here, in particular, never fail to impress me. He proposed to Gonne many times, but alas she was unattainable. I often wonder if Yeats hadn't fallen in love with Gonne, would we be left with a very different body of poetry.

NEVER GIVE ALL THE HEART

Never give all the heart, for love
Will hardly seem worth thinking of
To passionate women if it seem
Certain, and they never dream
That it fades out from kiss to kiss;
For everything that's lovely is
But a brief, dreamy, kind delight.
O never give the heart outright,
For they, for all smooth lips can say,
Have given their hearts up to the play.
And who could play it well enough
If deaf and dumb and blind with love?
He that made this knows all the cost,
For he gave all his heart and lost.

HER PRAISE

She is foremost of those that I would hear praised.
I have gone about the house, gone up and down
As a man does who has published a new book
Or a young girl dressed out in her new gown,
And though I have turned the talk by hook or crook
Until her praise should be the uppermost theme,
A woman spoke of some new tale she had read,
A man confusedly in a half dream
As though some other name ran in his head.
She is foremost of those that I would hear praised.
I will talk no more of books or the long war
But walk by the dry thorn until I have found
Some beggar sheltering from the wind, and there
Manage the talk until her name come round.
If there be rags enough he will know her name
And be well pleased remembering it, for in the old days,
Though she had young men's praise and old men's blame,
Among the poor both old and young gave her praise.

William Butler Yeats (1865–1939) was an Irish poet, widely considered one of the greatest poets of the twentieth century. Growing up between Dublin and Sligo, he was fascinated by Irish legends, a subject he would later explore in his work. A leading figure of the Irish literary establishment, he helped to found the Abbey Theatre, where he staged his play *Cathleen Ni Houlihan*. He was an influential forerunner of the Irish Literary Revival, along with Lady Gregory, Edward Martyn and others. His works include *The Wanderings of Oisín and Other Poems* (1889), *The Countess Cathleen and Various Legends and Lyrics* (1892) and *The Tower* (1928). He was appointed Senator for the Irish Free State in 1922 and, in 1923, he was awarded the Nobel Prize in Literature.

MARY DORCEY

ONE SUNDAY EVENING many years ago, I heard Mary Dorcey reading on stage at the Abbey Theatre. One of the pieces she read, and one I've selected here, was 'The Ordinary Woman'. She brought the house down. I went out the next morning to buy her poetry collection *Moving into the Space Cleared by Our Mothers*.

Some years later, I had the pleasure of launching Mary's novel, *Biography of Desire*, at the Irish Writers Centre in Parnell Square. It is the most amazing story of the love of one woman for another. I'd never heard anyone talking about it before and I don't think it ever got the full credit it deserved. But things are changing, and I'm so glad that women are now getting the recognition they deserve for their work in all areas of the arts.

WHEN YOU'RE ASLEEP

I'm worn out with you.

All day long
fetching and carrying
upstairs and downstairs
my back broken
picking up after you
forever under my feet.

Upstairs   downstairs
your questions trailing me
never quiet for two
minutes together –

How old were you the year that we went … ?
Do you remember the time
Somebody said … ?
Wasn't it grand the first
summer we saw … ?

Were you born yet

the last winter your father and I ... ?

Just let me tell you once more –

I know I've told you already ...

I'm worn out with you.

But for you these are festival

days;

days you can talk

all day long

out loud for a change

morning to night,

banqueting

because I'm here

to listen.

As the hours journey

from one meal to another

I hear my voice give out

an old litany:

Eat up now

stop talking
your food will be cold.
Mind the stairs
don't hurry ... you'll fall ...

Fasten your buttons
put on your slippers
watch where you're going
come on now – we're late ...
wash yourself quickly
get into bed
it's all hours already.
Pull up your covers ...
Yes –
I'll leave the door open ...
At last you're quiet
at last it's over –
all over again
until tomorrow
and I'm too tired
to kiss you or say goodnight.

Free –
I can go downstairs
read a book
or watch television.

I'm worn out with you.

Last of all
I look in
to see if you're sleeping –
your head sunk in the pillows
so still and so small ...
when did it grow so small?
I draw close
breath held
to catch yours –
and yes,
there it is –
softly, your mouth
almost smiling
the cat curled at your shoulder.

And I'm returned

thirty years or more

when I would call out

at night

as you closed the door

to hold you there

one moment longer.

Do you still love me?

I'd sing;

and back came the same answer

always –

When you're asleep!

RDINARY WOMAN

And again you ask me why –
Why don't I write a poem about
The ordinary woman?
Not the extreme, individual case,
But the normal woman, the average woman
The everyday woman?

The woman in the street
The woman in the field
The woman who works in a factory
The woman who works on a farm
The woman who has never heard of a factory
The woman who has never seen a field.

The woman who stays at home
The woman who has no home
The woman who raises children
The woman who can have no children

The woman who has too many children
The woman who wants no children.

The healthy woman   the sick woman
The growing woman   the dying woman
The menstruating woman   the menopausal woman
The woman on the make
The woman on the shelf.

The woman who works in a school
The woman who dropped out of school
The woman who never got into school.
The woman who works as a nurse
The woman who cooks for the nurse
The woman who cleans the kitchen

Where they cook for the nurse.
The woman who works in a shop every day
The woman who shops every day
The woman who shops for food
The woman who shops for clothes, for perfume
The woman who shoplifts

For clothes, for perfume.
The woman who is paid to catch
The woman who does not pay
For clothes   for food.
The career woman   the poetess woman
The mother earth woman   the charwoman

The amazon woman   the society woman
The sportswoman   the little woman
The woman who runs   the woman who walks
The woman who is on the run
The woman who has never walked.
The woman who drives a car

The woman who drives her husband's car.
The pampered woman   the kept woman
The sheltered woman   the battered woman
The victimised woman   the violent woman
The woman nobody wants
The woman who had it coming.

The woman who went sane

The woman who stayed mad

The woman who carries a gun

The woman who is shot by a gun

The woman with too much past

The woman with too little future.

The woman ahead of her times

The woman behind the times

The woman with no time.

The outdated rural woman

The alienated suburban woman

The overcrowded urban woman.

The woman who reads the news

The woman who has never made the news

The woman who starves herself to look right

The woman who starves.

The houseproud woman   the tinker woman

The family woman   the deserted woman

The illegitimate woman   the certified woman

The consumer woman   the alien woman

The emigrant woman   the immigrant woman

The decent woman   the fallen woman

The mother of his children   and

The other woman.

The articulate woman   the illiterate woman

The bluestocking woman   the ignorant woman

The deaf woman   the blind woman

The loud woman   the dumb woman

The big woman   the petite woman

The flatchested woman

The look at those tits woman

The ugly woman   the femme fatale woman

The feminine woman   the masculine woman

The painted woman   the naked woman

The lilywhite and the scarlet woman.

The woman who thinks too much

The woman who never had time to think.

The woman who fights the system

The woman who married the system

The woman who swims against the tide

The woman who swells the tide that drowns

The woman who swims against it.

The woman who sends her sons to kill

The sons of other women.

The woman who sees her daughters

Murdered by the sons of other women.

The woman who is capitalised

The woman who is communised

The woman who is colonised

The woman who is terrorised

The woman who is analysed

The woman who is advertised

The woman who is fertilised

The woman who is sterilised.

The woman who is locked in
The woman who is locked out
The woman in a prison cell
The woman in a convent cell
The woman who keeps her place
The woman who has no place.

The woman who loved her father too much
The woman who loved her mother too much
The woman who hates men
The woman who loves men
The woman who hates women
The woman who loves women.

The natural woman   the perverted woman
The veiled woman   the virgin woman
The celibate woman   the prostitute woman
The jewish woman   the buddhist muslim catholic
Hindu protestant woman
The french woman   the irish woman

The chinese woman   the indian woman

The african woman   the american woman.

The upperclass   upper middle class

Middle class   lower middle class

Upper working class   working class

Lower working class   the no class woman.

The who ever heard of her woman?

The who the hell is she woman?

The who the hell does she think she is woman?

The chaste woman   the frigid woman

The vamp the tramp and the nymphomaniac woman

The wholesome woman   the homely woman

The easy woman   the tight assed woman

The ball breaking   cock teasing

Doesn't know what she's made for woman.

The selfish woman   the martyred woman

The sluttish woman   the fussy woman

The loose woman   the uptight woman

The naive woman   the paranoid woman

The passive woman   the dominant woman

The silly woman   the hard woman

The placid woman   the angry woman

The sober woman   the drunken woman

The silent woman   the screaming woman

Yes, that's it – that's the one

Why don't you write a poem for her –

The ordinary woman?

Mary Dorcey (1950) is an Irish poet, short-story writer and novelist. In 1990, she won the Rooney Prize for Irish Literature for her short-story collection *A Noise from the Woodshed*. Having lived in Europe, the US and Japan, she has published eight previous books, including poetry, short-story and essay collections, and has been included in over one hundred anthologies. For many years, she led seminars at Trinity College Dublin's Centre for Gender and Women's Studies. She is a member of Aosdána and the Irish Academy of Writers and Artists.

PATRICK
KAVANAGH

WHEN I WAS younger, lots of my friends knew Patrick Kavanagh and were big admirers of his work. 'On Raglan Road' was one of my friend's favourite songs. I first encountered Kavanagh through reading his poetry and I absolutely loved 'A Christmas Childhood'. I think his work is beautiful.

Kavanagh is another poet who writes so well about the family. Indeed, the two poems I have selected here are about his relationships with his mother and father. I particularly admire the relationship he had with his mother. They seem to have been very close. I've long enjoyed the image of Kavanagh and his mother walking together 'in the oriental streets of thought'. What a lovely image.

I once did a reading at a Kavanagh festival in County Monaghan. They're great people to keep his memory going. I think it's so important for people to remember their own. Of course, Kavanagh meant a lot to many people. I was on a committee with the late Gus Martin of *Soundings* fame to bring back the Kavanagh papers to Ireland.

IN MEMORY OF MY MOTHER

I do not think of you lying in the wet clay
Of a Monaghan graveyard; I see
You walking down a lane among the poplars
On your way to the station, or happily

Going to second Mass on a summer Sunday –
You meet me and you say:
'Don't forget to see about the cattle – '
Among your earthiest words the angels stray.

And I think of you walking along a headland
Of green oats in June,
So full of repose, so rich with life –
And I see us meeting at the end of a town

On a fair day by accident, after
The bargains are all made and we can walk
Together through the shops and stalls and markets
Free in the oriental streets of thought.

O you are not lying in the wet clay,

For it is a harvest evening now and we

Are piling up the ricks against the moonlight

And you smile up at us – eternally.

MEMORY OF MY FATHER

Every old man I see
Reminds me of my father
When he had fallen in love with death
One time when sheaves were gathered.

That man I saw in Gardiner Street
Stumble on the kerb was one,
He stared at me half-eyed,
I might have been his son.

And I remember the musician
Faltering over his fiddle
In Bayswater, London.
He too set me the riddle.

Every old man I see
In October-coloured weather
Seems to say to me:
'I was once your father.'

Patrick Kavanagh (1904–1967) was a prolific Irish poet and novelist. Born in County Monaghan, he worked for years on the family farm before moving to Dublin to establish himself as a writer. His work is renowned and much loved for its accounts of rural Irish life and exploration of the commonplace. He is perhaps best known for his poems 'The Great Hunger' (1942) and 'On Raglan Road' (1946), and his novel *Tarry Flynn* (1948), based on his experiences as a young farmer. The Patrick Kavanagh Centre in Inniskeen, County Monaghan, regularly organises readings and exhibitions on Kavanagh and the local area.

EAVAN BOLAND

EAVAN BOLAND IS one of our greats. In the 1920s, women painters did not get the same recognition as the men – even though they were just as good as them. They were overlooked, and the same could be said of our women poets. I'm so glad now that so many women poets and artists are getting the attention they deserve.

Eavan and I spent five years on the Arts Council of Ireland together. She was always so beautifully mannered, with a great brain. She is currently a professor of English and Creative Writing at Stanford University.

Eavan told me herself that when she read her poem 'The Black Lace Fan My Mother Gave Me' to her mother for the first time, her mother stopped her to correct the price of the fan! You can see so clearly the scene of the beautiful lady waiting for this fine man. You can really feel the drama of the piece. I'm so happy to be able to include it here.

THE BLACK LACE FAN MY MOTHER GAVE ME

It was the first gift he ever gave her,
buying it for five francs in the *Galeries*
in pre-war Paris. It was stifling.
A starless drought made the nights stormy.

They stayed in the city for the summer.
They met in cafes. She was always early.
He was late. That evening he was later.
They wrapped the fan. He looked at his watch.

She looked down the Boulevard des Capucines.
She ordered more coffee. She stood up.
The streets were emptying. The heat was killing.
She thought the distance smelled of rain and lightning.

These are wild roses, appliqued on silk by hand,
darkly picked, stitched boldly, quickly.
The rest is tortoiseshell and has the reticent,
clear patience of its element. It is

a worn-out, underwater bullion and it keeps,
even now, an inference of its violation.
The lace is overcast as if the weather
it opened for and offset had entered it.

The past is an empty cafe terrace.
An airless dusk before thunder. A man running.
And no way to know what happened then –
none at all – unless, of course, you improvise:

The blackbird on this first sultry morning,
in summer, finding buds, worms, fruit,
feels the heat. Suddenly she puts out her wing –
the whole flirtatious span of it.

A BALLAD OF HOME

How we kissed
in our half-built house!
It was slightly timbered,
a bit bricked, on stilts

and we were newly married.
We drove out at dusk
and picked our way to safety
through flint and grit and brick.

Like water through a porthole,
the sky poured in.
We sat on one step
making estimations

and hugged until the watchman
called and cursed and swung
his waterproof torch
into our calculations.

Ten years on:
you wouldn't find now
an inch of spare ground.
Children in their cots,

books, a cat, plants
strain the walls' patience
and the last ounce of space.
And still every night

it all seems so sound.
But love why wouldn't it?
This house was built on our embrace
and there are worse foundations.

Eavan Boland (1944) is a poet and author, one of the foremost female voices in Irish literature. She was born in Dublin and studied in Ireland, London and New York. Her work is known for its appreciation of ordinary life, and interrogation of political and historical themes. She won a Jacob's Award in 1976. She has, over the years, been writer-in-residence at both Trinity College and University College Dublin, and poet-in-residence at the National Maternity Hospital, Dublin. Since 1996, she has been a tenured professor at Stanford University, where she is currently Melvin and Bill Lane Professor of English, and director of the creative writing programme.

SEAMUS HEANEY

SO MANY OF the poets in this collection have written about the family, and Seamus Heaney is no different. A few years ago, one of Seamus's poems, 'When all the others were away at Mass', was named Ireland's best-loved poem from the last century. It is a beautiful sonnet he wrote after the death of his mother. I love the two poems here because they are about his wife, Marie.

Seamus's skill, and indeed the skill of the other poets included in this collection, never ceases to amaze me. One line can say so much. All these poets want to do is write and put down their thoughts. But I often wonder if they ever really know how much it means to people – how much enjoyment we get from their writing.

I met Seamus on a number of occasions. He had a terrific sense of humour. He never sought out attention for himself and was always just part of the group. I stayed in a hotel with Seamus and Marie after the funeral of Brian Friel's daughter, Patricia. That evening, Marie told me about when they arrived back in Dublin after Seamus received the Nobel Prize in 1995. The red carpet had been rolled out to the steps of the aircraft and there were lots of people waiting below, including their children. That must have been some moment!

TWICE SHY

Her scarf a la Bardot,
In suede flats for the walk,
She came with me one evening
For air and friendly talk.
We crossed the quiet river,
Took the embankment walk.

Traffic holding its breath,
Sky a tense diaphragm:
Dusk hung like a backcloth
That shook where a swan swam,
Tremulous as a hawk
Hanging deadly, calm.

A vacuum of need
Collapsed each hunting heart
But tremulously we held
As hawk and prey apart,

Preserved classic decorum,
Deployed our talk with art.

Our Juvenilia
Had taught us both to wait,
Not to publish feeling
And regret it all too late –
Mushroom loves already
Had puffed and burst in hate.

So, chary and excited,
As a thrush linked on a hawk,
We thrilled to the March twilight
With nervous childish talk:
Still waters running deep
Along the embankment walk.

VALEDICTION

Lady with the frilled blouse
And simple tartan skirt,
Since you left the house
Its emptiness has hurt
All thought. In your presence
Time rode easy, anchored
On a smile; but absence
Rocked love's balance, unmoored
The days. They buck and bound
Across the calendar,
Pitched from the quiet sound
Of your flower-tender
Voice. Need breaks on my strand;
You've gone, I am at sea.
Until you resume command,
Self is in mutiny.

Seamus Heaney (1939–2013) was a renowned Irish poet, playwright and translator. Educated at Queen's University Belfast, he worked as a schoolteacher and college lecturer before publishing his first major poetry collection, *Death of a Naturalist*, in 1966. Since then, he published many acclaimed collections including *North* (1975), *Field Work* (1979) and *District and Circle* (2006). As a translator, Heaney published a highly regarded translation of *Beowulf* in 1999. In 1995, he was awarded the Nobel Prize in Literature. He also won two Whitbread Prizes (1996, 1999), the T.S. Eliot Prize (2006) and, in 1998, was elected Saoi of Aosdána.

CAROL ANN DUFFY

I ONCE HEARD Carol Ann Duffy read in Cleere's Pub in Kilkenny at the festival there some years ago. Cleere's Pub was a very cosy setting, with everyone sitting close to her. It was almost like a drawing-room situation.

Carol Ann, one of our own (her mother was Irish and her father had Irish grandparents), introduced each poem that evening with a wonderful story or anecdote, beautifully spoken and oh so funny and entertaining. She was so witty and off the cuff; she never faltered, just spoke to everyone comfortably. It was outstanding. People came out of there on a high.

I was so excited by her that I thought Gay must have her on *The Late Late Show*. They tried very hard but, unfortunately, she was too busy. I wonder would we have enjoyed the performance as much in a bigger venue. It was such a special evening and one of the greatest moments of my life – I will never forget it.

'Text' is probably the most up-to-date poem in this book. It hits the nail on the head as to where the world is now. It's so clear and she gets her message across quickly in a few short lines.

TEA

I like pouring your tea, lifting
the heavy pot, and tipping it up,
so the fragrant liquid steams in your china cup.

Or when you're away, or at work,
I like to think of your cupped hands as you sip,
as you sip, of the faint half-smile of your lips.

I like the questions – sugar? milk? –
and the answers I don't know by heart, yet,
for I see your soul in your eyes, and I forget.

Jasmine, Gunpowder, Assam, Earl Grey, Ceylon,
I love tea's names. Which tea would you like? I say,
but it's any tea, for you, please, any time of the day,

as the women harvest the slopes,
for the sweetest leaves, on Mount Wu-Yi,
and I am your lover, smitten, straining your tea.

TEXT

I tend the mobile now
like an injured bird.

We text, text, text
our significant words.

I re-read your first,
your second, your third,

look for your small *xx*,
feeling absurd.

The codes we send
arrive like a broken chord.

I try to picture your hands,
their image is blurred.

Nothing my thumbs press
will ever be heard.

Carol Ann Duffy (1955) is a poet and playwright from Scotland. She lives in Manchester, where she is Professor and Creative Director of the Writing School at Manchester Metropolitan University. She has written for both adults and children. Her work has received numerous awards including the Dylan Thomas Prize (1989), the Whitbread Award (1993), a Lannan Award (1995) and the T.S. Eliot Prize (2005). She was appointed Britain's Poet Laureate in 2009, the first woman to hold the position.

FRANCIS
LEDWIDGE

IN A FITTING tribute to Francis Ledwidge, Seamus Heaney once referred to the poet as 'our dead enigma'. While certainly true, much of Ledwidge's work has touched me throughout my life. I always find it so interesting when poets write about the family – how they capture quiet, everyday instances we can all relate to and understand. Indeed, one of the poems I have selected here concerns the family.

I remember the first time I read 'My Mother', particularly the line, "For there is that in her which always mourns". I remember thinking to myself: that's my mother he's writing about. It's exactly what I observed at home when I was a child, because my parents had lost three children. The description and emotion captured is so accurate and beautiful.

Heaney went on to describe Ledwidge as a 'tender beautiful figure, walking in a mist of melancholy' – what a stirring image.

MY MOTHER

God made my mother on an April day,
From sorrow and the mist along the sea,
Lost birds' and wanderers' songs and ocean spray,
And the moon loved her wandering jealously.

Beside the ocean's din she combed her hair,
Singing the nocturne of the passing ships,
Before her earthly lover found her there
And kissed away the music from her lips.

She came unto the hills and saw the change
That brings the swallow and the geese in turns.
But there was not a grief she deeméd strange,
For there is that in her which always mourns.

Kind heart she has for all on hill or wave
Whose hopes grew wings like ants to fly away.
I bless the God who such a mother gave
This poor bird-hearted singer of a day.

LAMENT FOR THOMAS MACDONAGH

He shall not hear the bittern cry
In the wild sky, where he is lain,
Nor voices of the sweeter birds,
Above the wailing of the rain.

Nor shall he know when loud March blows
Thro' slanting snows her fanfare shrill,
Blowing to flame the golden cup
Of many an upset daffodil.

But when the Dark Cow leaves the moor,
And pastures poor with greedy weeds,
Perhaps he'll hear her low at morn,
Lifting her horn in pleasant meads.

Francis Ledwidge (1887–1917) was an Irish war poet, sometimes known as the 'Poet of the Blackbirds'. After publishing some work in local newspapers, he caught the attention of Lord Dunsany, who became his patron and introduced him to likes of W.B. Yeats and Lady Gregory. Politically active, he became secretary of the Meath Ulster Union and, in 1914, joined an Irish regiment in support of the Allied war cause. His first collection, *Songs of the Field* – the only of his lifetime – was published in 1915. Ledwidge was killed at Ypres in 1917. He was twenty-nine years old. Dunsany later arranged for more of his work to be published, including *Last Songs* (1918) and *The Complete Poems of Francis Ledwidge* (1919).

PAULA MEEHAN

AS I'VE SAID, for me the best poetry paints a picture, and Paula Meehan does this so well. I once saw her give a reading at St Canice's Cathedral in Kilkenny. She read 'The Pattern', which is one of the poems I've selected here. She went down so well on the night – her pace and her diction were just perfect. She left us wanting more.

'The Pattern' is such a real piece. The narrator has all the things from her mother's life but not enough of her love. You can feel her desire for her mother to love her. It's a real painting – you can visualise the woman remembering and looking back, surrounded by her things.

'My Father Perceived as a Vision of St Francis', the second poem I've included, reminds me of a man I regularly see in Herbert Park, who has huge pockets full of bread. The birds sit on his head and shoulders, and on his hat. If he holds out his arms, they alight on them. It's an extraordinary performance to see him feed the birds, the doves flying all around him. If you were to arrange it artistically you couldn't do it better – it's a beautiful sight. One day I brought lots of bread to the park to try and imitate him but it didn't work – the birds only have time for him!

THE PATTERN

Little has come down to me of hers,
a sewing machine, a wedding band,
a clutch of photos, the sting of her hand
across my face in one our wars

when we had grown bitter and apart.
Some say that's the fate of the eldest daughter.
I wish now she'd lasted till after
I'd grown up. We might have made a new start

as women without tags like *mother*, *wife*,
sister, *daughter*, taken our chances from there.
At forty-two she headed for god knows where.
I've never gone back to visit her grave.

*

First she'd scrub the floor with Sunlight soap,
an armreach at a time. When her knees grew sore

she'd break for a cup of tea, then start again
at the door with lavender polish. The smell
would percolate back through the flat to us,
her brood banished to the bedroom.

And as she buffed the wax to a high shine
did she catch her own face coming clear?
Did she net a glimmer of her true self?
Did her mirror tell her what mine tells me?

I have her shrug and go on
knowing history has brought her to her knees.

She'd call us in and let us skate around
in our socks. We'd grow solemn as planets
in an intricate orbit about her.

*

She's bending over crimson cloth,
the younger kids are long in bed.
Late summer. Cold enough for a fire,

she works by fading light

to remake an old dress for me.

It's first day back at school tomorrow.

*

'Pure lambswool. Plenty of wear in it yet.

You know I wore this when I went out with your Da.

I was supposed to be down in a friend's house,

your Granda caught us at the corner.

He dragged me in by the hair – it was long as yours then –

in front of the whole street.

He called your Da every name under the sun,

cornerboy, lout; I needn't tell you

what he called me. He shoved my whole head

under the kitchen tap, took a scrubbing brush

and carbolic soap and in ice-cold water he scrubbed

every speck of lipstick and mascara off my face.

Christ but he was a right tyrant, your Granda.

It'll be over my dead body that anyone harms a hair on

    your head.'

*

She must have stayed up half the night
to finish the dress. I found it airing at the fire,
three new copybooks on the table and a bright
bronze nib, St Christopher strung on a silver wire,

as if I were embarking on a perilous journey
to uncharted realms. I wore that dress
with little grace. To me it spelt poverty,
the stigma of the second hand. I grew enough to pass

it on by Christmas to the next in line. I was sizing
up the world beyond our flat patch by patch
daily after school, and fitting each surprising
city street to city square to diamond. I'd watch

the Liffey for hours pulsing to the sea
and the coming and going of ships,
certain that one day it would carry me
to Zanzibar, Bombay, the land of the Ethiops.

*

There's a photo of her taken in the Phoenix Park
alone on a bench surrounded by roses
as if she had been born to formal gardens.
She stares out as if unaware
that any human hand held the camera, wrapped
entirely in her own shadow, the world beyond her
already a dream, already lost. She's
eight months pregnant. Her last child.

*

Her steel needles sparked and clacked,
the only other sound a settling coal
or her sporadic mutter
at a hard part in the pattern.
She favoured sensible shades:
Moss Green, Mustard, Beige.

I dreamt a robe of a colour
so pure it became a word.

Sometimes I'd have to kneel
an hour before her by the fire,
a skein around my outstretched hands,
while she rolled wool into balls.
If I swam like a kite too high
amongst the shadows on the ceiling
or flew like a fish in the pools
of pulsing light, she'd reel me firmly
home, she'd land me at her knees.

Tongues of flame in her dark eyes,
she'd say, 'One of these days I must
teach you to follow a pattern.'

MY FATHER PERCEIVED AS A VISION OF ST FRANCIS

for Brendan Kennelly

It was the piebald horse in next door's garden

frightened me out of a dream

with her dawn whinny. I was back

in the boxroom of the house,

my brother's room now,

full of ties and sweaters and secrets.

Bottles chinked on the doorstep,

the first bus pulled up to the stop.

The rest of the house slept

except for my father. I heard

him rake the ash from the grate,

plug in the kettle, hum a snatch of a tune.

Then he unlocked the back door

and stepped out into the garden.

Autumn was nearly done, the first frost

whitened the slates of the estate.

He was older than I had reckoned,

his hair completely silver,
and for the first time I saw the stoop
of his shoulder, saw that
his leg was stiff. What's he at?
So early and still stars in the west?

They came then: birds
of every size, shape, colour; they came
from the hedges and shrubs,
from eaves and garden sheds,
from the industrial estate, outlying fields,
from Dubber Cross they came
and the ditches of the North Road.
The garden was a pandemonium
when my father threw up his hands
and tossed the crumbs to the air. The sun

cleared O'Reilly's chimney
and he was suddenly radiant,
a perfect vision of St Francis,
made whole, made young again,
in a Finglas garden.

Paula Meehan (1955) was born in Dublin. She studied at Trinity College, Dublin, and Eastern Washington University, where she would later become a teaching fellow. After travelling extensively, she has published widely across both poetry and the stage, often collaborating with artists, musicians and film-makers. She is also involved with arts projects with prisoners and local communities. In 2013, she was instated as the Ireland Professor of Poetry by President Michael D. Higgins and, in 2015, she was inducted into the Hennessy Literary Awards Hall of Fame for her achievements in poetry. She is a member of Aosdána.

PADRAIC COLUM

ONE OF MY first meetings with a renowned poet came in the early days of Radio Telefís Éireann, where I worked as one of the first continuity announcers. A rumour went around that Padraic Colum was coming into the studio for an interview. Of course there was great excitement because everybody, myself included, had studied his poems at school. From the time I was very young I had loved his work – he was the first poet to get to me growing up as a child.

Just before they started recording, I noticed a horn of hair sticking out from the middle of his head, as if it were lacquered into place. It was quickly decided that someone had better tell him – it was dreadful looking. There was a bit of hushed elbowing – 'You tell him. No, you tell him!' – so I went in and said, 'Excuse me, Mr Colum, we can't let you go on air because your hair is sticking up in the middle and we have to do something about it.' He said to me, 'Would you put it down for me?', so I can now say that with both hands I smoothed down the head of a famous poet!

'An Old Woman of the Roads' brings back so many memories to me. It pictures exactly what you saw in early twentieth-century Ireland. The country people all had the dresser and the clock and the very colourful jugs and bowls. We were delighted when our mother would break a cup as we'd play with the bits of broken delph and china – we called them chainies. We had more fun with them than I can tell you. At that time in the countryside you made your own play – nothing was bought.

My mother's friend, Mrs Dunne, had a gorgeous open fire, with the big black ironwork and a big skillet pot hanging up – it was really very beautiful. The drover was also a common sight; I can still see the cattle being herded, bringing cows along the road from one field to another.

All those things were part of a magical childhood in the country, when life was free and easy and you were playing in the fields and the hedges.

AN OLD WOMAN OF THE ROADS

O, to have a little house!
To own the hearth and stool and all!
The heaped up sods upon the fire,
The pile of turf against the wall!

To have a clock with weights and chains
And pendulum swinging up and down!
A dresser filled with shining delph,
Speckled and white and blue and brown!

I could be busy all the day
Clearing and sweeping hearth and floor,
And fixing on their shelf again
My white and blue and speckled store!

I could be quiet there at night
Beside the fire and by myself,
Sure of a bed and loth to leave
The ticking clock and the shining delph!

Och! but I'm weary of mist and dark,

And roads where there's never a house nor bush,

And tired I am of bog and road,

And the crying wind and the lonesome hush!

And I am praying to God on high,

And I am praying Him night and day,

For a little house – a house of my own –

Out of the wind's and the rain's way.

A DROVER

To Meath of the pastures,
From wet hills by the sea,
Through Leitrim and Longford
Go my cattle and me.

I hear in the darkness
Their slipping and breathing.
I name them the bye-ways
They're to pass without heeding.

Then the wet, winding roads,
Brown bogs with black water;
And my thoughts on white ships
And the King o' Spain's daughter.

O! farmer, strong farmer!
You can spend at the fair
But your face you must turn
To your crops and your care.

And soldiers – red soldiers!
You've seen many lands;
But you walk two by two,
And by captain's commands.

O! the smell of the beasts,
The wet wind in the morn;
And the proud and hard earth
Never broken for corn;

And the crowds at the fair,
The herds loosened and blind,
Loud words and dark faces
And the wild blood behind.

(O! strong men with your best
I would strive breast to breast
I could quiet your herds
With my words, with my words.)

I will bring you, my kine,

Where there's grass to the knee;

But you'll think of scant croppings

Harsh with salt of the sea.

Padraic Colum (1881–1972) was an Irish poet, novelist, folklorist, children's writer and playwright. A leading figure of the Irish Literary Revival, he was an active member of both the National Theatre Society and the Abbey Theatre, where he collaborated with the likes of James Joyce, W.B. Yeats and Lady Gregory. He published prolifically throughout his lifetime across poetry, fiction, nonfiction, folklore, children's literature and drama, including the plays *The Land* (1905) and *Thomas Muskerry* (1910), and the poetry collections *Dramatic Legends* (1922) and *Creatures* (1927). He later taught at Columbia University. He died in 1972.

ACKNOWLEDGEMENTS

The publishers gratefully acknowledge permission to reprint copyright material in this book as follows:

Poems by Brendan Kennelly taken from *Familiar Strangers: New and Selected Poems 1960–2004* (Bloodaxe Books, 2004), reproduced with permission of Bloodaxe Books. www.bloodaxebooks.com.

Poems by Rita Ann Higgins included by kind permission of the author and Salmon Poetry, 9 Parliament Street, Ennistymon, Co. Clare.

Poems by Mary Dorcey taken from *To Air the Soul, Throw All the Windows Wide: New and Selected Poems* (Salmon Poetry, 2016), included by kind permission of the author and Salmon Poetry, 9 Parliament Street, Ennistymon, Co. Clare.

Poems by Patrick Kavanagh reprinted from *Collected Poems*, edited by Antoinette Quinn (Allen Lane, 2004), by kind permission of the Trustees of the Estate of the late Katherine B. Kavanagh, through the Jonathan Williams Literary Agency.

Poems by Eavan Boland taken from *New Collected Poems* (Carcanet, 2005), reproduced with permission of Carcanet Press, 4th floor, Alliance House, 30 Cross Street, Manchester M2 7AQ.

Poems by Seamus Heaney taken from *Death of a Naturalist* (Faber & Faber, 2006), reproduced with permission of Faber & Faber, Bloomsbury House, 74–77 Great Russell Street, London WC1B 3DA.

Poems by Carol Ann Duffy taken from *Love Poems* (Picador, 2010), reproduced with permission of Pan Macmillan, 20 New Wharf Road, London NI 9RR.

Poems by Paula Meehan included by kind permission of the author and Dedalus Press, 13 Moyclare Road, Baldoyle, Dublin 13.

Poems by Padraic Colum included by kind permission of the Estate of Padraic Colum.